No Such Thing as Too Big a Dream

A book of powerful and inspirational quotes

No Such Thing as Too Big a Dream:
A book of powerful and inspirational quotes
By **J. Recinos**

To Dani,

for showing me that no dream is too big.

Te adoro.

Contents

Chapter 1

Attitude Quotes

"To be a great champion you must believe you are the best. If you're not, pretend you are."
Muhammad Ali

"Attitude is a little thing that makes a big difference."
Sir Winston Churchill

"To different minds, the same world is a hell, and a heaven."
Ralph Waldo Emerson

"Everyone has his burden. What counts is how you carry it."
Merle Miller

"Weakness of attitude becomes weakness of character"
Albert Einstein

"The only disability in life is a bad attitude"
Scott Hamilton

"If you don't like something, change it. If you can't change it, change your attitude."
Maya Angelou

"Nothing can stop the man with the right mental attitude from achieving his goal; nothing on earth can help the man with the wrong mental attitude."
Thomas Jefferson

"Excellence is not a skill. It is an attitude"
Ralph Marston

"Finish each day and be done with it. You have done what you could. Some blunders and absurdities no doubt crept in; forget them as soon as you can. Tomorrow is a new day; begin it well and serenely and with too high a spirit to be cumbered with your old nonsense."
Ralph Waldo Emerson

"Happiness is not by chance, but by choice."
Jim Rohn

"Character is the result of two things: mental attitude and the way we spend our time."
Elbert Green Hubbard

"I've got to say "no" to the good so I can say "yes" to the best."
Zig Ziglar

"Determine the thing that can and shall be done, and then we shall find the way."
Abraham Lincoln

"Whether you think you can, or think you can't, you're right"
Henry Ford

"Become a possibilitarian. No matter how dark things seem to be or actually are, raise your sights and see possibilities - always see them, for they're always there."
Norman Vincent Peale

"Be not afraid of life. Believe that life is worth living and your belief will help create the fact."
William James

"Oh, my friend, it's not what they take away from you that counts. It's what you do with what you have left."
Hubert Humphrey

Chapter 2

Determination Quotes

"Success is not final, failure is not fatal: it is the courage to continue that counts"
Sir Winston Churchill

"The difference between the impossible and the possible lies in a person's determination."
Tommy Lasorda

"We will either find a way, or make one!"
Hannibal

"Obstacles don't have to stop you. If you run into a wall, don't turn around and give up. Figure out how to climb it, go through it, or work around it."
Michael Jordan

"I am not discouraged, because every wrong attempt discarded is another step forward."
Thomas Alva Edison

"What this power is I cannot say; all I know is that it exists and it becomes available only when a man is in that state of mind in which he knows exactly what he wants and is fully determined not to quit until he finds it."
Alexander Graham Bell

"It's a very funny thing about life; if you refuse to accept anything but the best, you very often get it."
William Somerset Maugham

"Determination is the wake-up call to the human will."
Anthony Robbins

"You have to learn the rules of the game and then you have to play better than anyone else"
Albert Einstein

"Little by little one walks far"
Peruvian Proverb

"Keep your dreams alive. Understand to achieve
anything requires faith and belief in yourself, vision,
hard work, determination, and dedication. Remember
all things are possible for those who believe."
Gail Devers

"You've got to get up every morning with determination
if you're going to go to bed with satisfaction."
George Lorimer

"When you get into a tight place and everything goes against you, till it seems as though you could not hold on a minute longer, never give up then, for that is just the place and time that the tide will turn."
Harriet Beecher Stowe

"If you don't have the time to do it right when will you have the time to do it over?"
John Wooden

"There is no chance, no destiny, no fate that can circumvent or hinder or control the firm resolve of a determined soul."
Ella Wheeler Wilcox

"Some are destined to succeed, some are determined
to succeed."
H. H. Swami Tejomayananda

"When the sun is shining I can do anything; no
mountain is too high, no trouble too difficult to
overcome."
Wilma Rudolph

"When faced with a mountain, I will not quit! I will keep
striving until I climb over, find a pass through, tunnel
underneath or simply stay and turn the mountain into a
gold mine, with God's help."
Robert Half

Chapter 3

Dream Quotes

"Man, alone, has the power to transform his thoughts into physical reality; man, alone, can dream and make his dreams come true."
Napoleon Hill

"You see things; and you say, 'Why?' But I dream things that never were; and I say, 'Why not?'"
George Bernard Shaw

"The future belongs to those that believe in the beauty of their dreams"
Eleanor Roosevelt

"Happy are those who dream dreams and are willing to pay the price to make them come true."
Anonymous

"Go confidently in the direction of your dreams. Live the life you have imagined."
Henry David Thoreau

"Hold fast to dreams, for if dreams die, life is a broken winged bird that cannot fly."
Langston Hughes

"Commitment leads to action. Action brings your dream closer."
Marcia Wieder

"What is not started today is never finished tomorrow"
Johann Wolfgang Von Goethe

"The only thing that will stop you from fulfilling your dreams is you"
Tom Bradley

"Dreams are renewable. No matter what our age or condition, there are still untapped possibilities within us and new beauty waiting to be born."
Dr. Dale E. Turner

"We should show life neither as it is nor as it ought to be, but only as we see it in our dreams."
Count Leo Tolstoy

"However vague they are, dreams have a way of concealing themselves and leave us no peace until they are translated into reality, like seeds germinating underground, sure to sprout in their search for the sunlight."
Lin Yutang

"Dreams are illustrations from the book your soul is writing about you."
Marsha Norman

"Dreams are today's answers to tomorrow's questions"
Edgar Cayce

"You are never too old to set another goal or to dream a new dream."
C.S Lewis

"Whatever you do, or dream you can, begin it.
Boldness has genius and power and magic in it."
Johann Wolfgang von Goethe

"All men dream but not equally. Those who dream by
night in the dusty recesses of their minds wake in the
day to find that it was vanity but the dreamers of the
day are dangerous men, for they may act their dreams
with open eyes, to make it possible."
T.E Lawrence

"To dream anything that you want to dream. That's the
beauty of the human mind. To do anything that you
want to do. That is the strength of the human will. To
trust yourself to test your limits. That is the courage to
succeed."
Bernard Edmonds

Chapter 4

Fear of Failure Quotes

"I failed my way to success."
Thomas Alva Edison

"I was never afraid of failure, for I would sooner fail
than not be among the best."
John Keats

"There is no impossibility to him who stands prepared
to conquer every hazard. The fearful are the failing."
Sarah J. Hale

"Our doubts are traitors, and make us lose the good we oft might win, by fearing to attempt."
William Shakespeare

"Every failure brings with it the seed of an equivalent success."
Napoleon Hill

"One who fears failure limits his activities. Failure is only the opportunity to more intelligently begin again."
Henry Ford

What would life be if we had no courage to attempt anything?
Vincent van Gogh

"There are no failures - just experiences and your reactions to them."
Tom Krause

"Try and fail, but don't fail to try."
Stephen Kaggwa

"Failure is a detour, not a dead-end street."
Zig Ziglar

"Failure is the tuition you pay for success."
Walter Brunell

"Failure is not falling down but refusing to get up."
Chinese Proverb

"You'll always miss 100% of the shots you don't take."
Wayne Gretzky

"Failure is nature's plan to prepare you for great responsibilities"
Napoleon Hill

"To fail is a natural consequence of trying, to succeed takes time and prolonged effort in the face of unfriendly odds. To think it will be any other way, no matter what you do, is to invite yourself to be hurt and to limit your enthusiasm for trying"
David Viscott

"Failure is success if we learn from it."
Malcolm S. Forbes

"Don't fear failure so much that you refuse to try new things. The saddest summary of a life contains three descriptions: could have, might have and should have."
Louis E. Boone

"Inaction breeds doubt and fear. Action breeds confidence and courage. If you want to conquer fear, do not sit home and think about it. Go out and get busy."
Dale Carnegie

Chapter 5

Goal Quotes

"The more intensely we feel about an idea or a goal, the more assuredly the idea, buried deep in our subconscious, will direct us along the path to its fulfillment."
Earl Nightingale

"There is no happiness except in the realization that we have accomplished something."
Henry Ford

"Who aims at excellence will be above mediocrity; who aims at mediocrity will be far short of it."
Burmese Saying

"There are two things to aim at in life; first to get what you want, and after that to enjoy it. Only the wisest of mankind has achieved the second."
Logan Pearsall Smith

"The major reason for setting a goal is for what it makes of you to accomplish it. What it makes of you will always be the far greater value than what you get."
Jim Rohn

"Any person who selects a goal in life which can be fully achieved, has already defined his own limitations"
Cavett Robert

"People with goals succeed because they know where they are going. It's as simple as that."
Earl Nightingale

"By prevailing over all obstacles and distractions, one may unfailingly arrive at his chosen goal or destination."
Christopher Columbus

"Begin with the end in mind."
Stephen Covey

"Some of the world's greatest feats were accomplished by people not smart enough to know they were impossible."
Doug Larson

"The question isn't who is going to let me; it's who is going to stop me."
Ayn Rand

"It is never too late to be who you might have been."
George Elliot

"How am I going to live today in order to create the tomorrow I'm committed to?"
Anthony Robbins

"I find it fascinating that most people plan their vacation with better care than they do their lives. Perhaps that is because escape is easier than change."
Jim Rohn

"If you have built castles in the air, your work need not be lost; that is where they should be. Now put the foundations under them."
Henry David Thoreau

"Map out your future, but do it in pencil."
Jon Bon Jovi

"Every day you spend drifting away from your goals is a waste not only of that day, but also of the additional day it takes to regain lost ground"
Ralph Marston

"When people say to me: "How do you do so many things?" I often answer them, without meaning to be cruel: "How do you do so little?" It seems to me that people have vast potential. Most people can do extraordinary things if they have the confidence or take the risks. Yet most people don't. They sit in front of the telly and treat life as if it goes on forever."
Philip Adams

Chapter 6

Happiness Quotes

"Happiness is the meaning and the purpose of life, the whole aim and end of human existence"
Aristotle

"There is only one success - to spend your life in your own way."
-Christopher Morley

"Success is not the key to happiness. Happiness is the key to success. If you love what you are doing, you will be successful."
Herman Cain

"Don't rely on someone else for your happiness and self worth. Only you can be responsible for that. If you can't love and respect yourself - no one else will be able to make that happen. Accept who you are - completely; the good and the bad - and make changes as YOU see fit - not because you think someone else wants you to be different."
Stacey Charter

"Happiness resides not in possessions and not in gold, the feeling of happiness dwells in the soul."
Democritus

"Be happy while you're living, for you're a long time dead"
Scottish Proverb

"Sooner or later in life everyone discovers that perfect happiness is unrealizable, but there are few who pause to consider the antithesis: that perfect unhappiness is equally unattainable."
Primo Levi

"The happiness of life is made up of minute fractions—the little soon-forgotten charities of a kiss, a smile, a kind look, a heartfelt compliment in the disguise of a playful raillery, and the countless other infinitesimals of pleasurable thought and genial feeling."
Samuel Taylor Coleridge

"Happiness comes of the capacity to feel deeply, to enjoy simply, to think freely, to risk life, to be needed."
Storm Jameson

"Happiness comes of the capacity to feel deeply, to enjoy simply, to think freely, to risk life, to be needed."
Maxim Gorky

"Even if happiness forgets you a little bit, never completely forget about it."
Jacques Prévert

"A string of excited, fugitive, miscellaneous pleasures is not happiness; happiness resides in imaginative reflection and judgment, when the picture of one's life, or of human life, as it truly has been or is, satisfies the will, and is gladly accepted."
George Santayana

"Don't limit investing to the financial world. Invest something of yourself, and you will be richly rewarded."
Charles Schwab

"Nobody really cares if you're miserable, so you might as well be happy."
Cynthia Nelms

"There is only one way to achieve happiness on this terrestrial ball,
And that is to have either a clear conscience or none at all."
Ogden Nash

"Each morning when I open my eyes I say to myself: I, not events, have the power to make me happy or unhappy today. I can choose which it shall be. Yesterday is dead, tomorrow hasn't arrived yet. I have just one day, today, and I'm going to be happy in it."
Groucho Marx

"Happiness is a perfume you cannot pour on others without getting a few drops on yourself."
Ralph Waldo Emerson

"If you want to be happy, be."
Leo Tolstoy

Chapter 7

Inspirational Quotes

"Every artist was first an amateur."
Ralph Waldo Emerson

"Your time is limited, so don't waste it living someone else's life. Don't be trapped by dogma - which is living with the results of other people's thinking. Don't let the noise of other's opinions drown out your own inner voice. And most important, have the courage to follow your heart and intuition. They somehow already know what you truly want to become. Everything else is secondary."
Steve Jobs

"Try not to become a man of success but a man of value."
Albert Einstein

"Courage doesn't always roar. Sometimes courage is the quiet voice at the end of the day saying, "I will try again tomorrow."
Mary Anne Radmacher

"First say to yourself what you would be; and then do what you have to do."
Epictetus

"Man cannot discover new oceans unless he has the courage to lose sight of the shore."
Andre Gide

"The most powerful weapon on earth is the human soul on fire."
Ferdinand Foch

"It's kind of fun to do the impossible."
Walt Disney

"The ultimate measure of a man is not where he stands in moments of comfort, but where he stands at times of challenge and controversy."
Martin Luther King Jr.

"If you are going through hell, keep going."
Sir Winston Churchill

"Live as if you were to die tomorrow. Learn as if you were to live forever."
Mahatma Gandhi

"Don't listen to anyone who tells you that you can't do this or that. That's nonsense. Make up your mind, you'll never use crutches or a stick, then have a go at everything. Go to school; join in all the games you can. Go anywhere you want to. But never, never let them persuade you that things are too difficult or impossible."
Douglas Bader

"Happy are those who dream dreams and are ready to pay the price to make them come true."
Leon J. Suenes

"The tragedy of life is not that it ends so soon, but that we wait so long to begin it."
W. M. Lewis

"For every dark night, there's a brighter day"
Tupac Shakur

"Inspiration exists, but it has to find us working"
Pablo Picasso

"And in the end, it's not the years in your life that count. It's the life in your years."
Abraham Lincoln

"Everything you can imagine is real"
Pablo Picasso

Chapter 8

Obstacles Quotes

"If you can find a path with no obstacles, it probably doesn't lead anywhere."
Frank A. Clark

"The block of granite which was an obstacle in the pathway of the weak becomes a stepping-stone in the pathway of the strong"
Thomas Carlyle

"A hero is an ordinary individual who finds the strength to persevere and endure in spite of overwhelming obstacles."
Christopher Reeve

"History has demonstrated that the most notable winners usually encountered heartbreaking obstacles before they triumphed. They won because they refused to become discouraged by their defeats."
B. C. Forbes

"Obstacles are like wild animals. They are cowards but they will bluff you if they can. If they see you are afraid of them, they are liable to spring upon you; but if you look them squarely in the eye, they will slink out of sight."
Orison Swett Marden

"Most of our obstacles would melt away if, instead of cowering before them, we should make up our minds to walk boldly through them."
Orison Swett Marden

"The majority sees the obstacles; the few see the objectives; history records the successes of the latter, while oblivion is the reward of the former."
Alfred A. Montapert

"Stand up to your obstacles and do something about them. You will find that they haven't half the strength you think they have."
Norman Vincent Peale

"One who gains strength by overcoming obstacles possesses the only strength which can overcome adversity."
Albert Schweitzer

"Wanting something is not enough. You must hunger for it. Your motivation must be absolutely compelling in order to overcome the obstacles that will invariably come your way."
Les Brown

"If you are not criticized, you may not be doing much."
Donald H. Rumsfeld

"Yesterday I dared to struggle. Today I dare to win."
Bernadette Devlin

"Let a person rejoice when he is confronted with obstacles, for it means that he has reached the end of some particular line of indifference or folly, and is now called upon to summon up all his energy and intelligence in order to extricate himself, and to find a better way; that the powers within him are crying out for greater freedom, for enlarged exercise and scope."
James Allen

"If we had no winter, the spring would not be so pleasant; if we did not sometimes taste of adversity, prosperity would not be so welcome."
Anne Bradstreet

"The way I see it, if you want the rainbow, you gotta put up with the rain."
Dolly Parton

"There are two kinds of people in the world: those who make excuses and those who get results. An excuse person will find any excuse for why a job was not done, and a results person will find any reason why it can be done. Be a creator, not a reactor."
Alan Cohen

"But I firmly believe that any man's finest hour, his greatest fulfillment of all he holds dear, is the moment when he has worked his heart out in a good cause and lies exhausted on the field of battle - victorious."
Vince Lombardi

"You don't drown by falling in the water; you drown by staying there."
Edwin Louis Cole

Chapter 9

Optimism Quotes

"A pessimist sees the difficulty in every opportunity; an optimist sees the opportunity in every difficulty."
Sir Winston Churchill

"Having a positive mental attitude is asking how something can be done rather than saying it can't be done."
Bo Bennett

"Between the optimist and the pessimist, the difference is droll. The optimist sees the doughnut; the pessimist the hole!"
Oscar Wilde

"Optimism is the faith that leads to achievement.
Nothing can be done without hope and confidence."
Helen Keller

"If you realized how powerful your thoughts are, you
would never think a negative thought."
Peace Pilgrim

"I'm not afraid of storms, for I'm learning how to sail
my ship."
Louisa May Alcott

"I'm not afraid of storms, for I'm learning how to sail my ship."
Kahlil Gibran

"Pessimism leads to weakness, optimism to power"
William James

"Enter every activity without giving mental recognition to the possibility of defeat. Concentrate on your strengths, instead of your weaknesses... on your powers, instead of your problems."
Paul J Meyer

"An optimist stays up until midnight to see the new year in. A pessimist stays up to make sure the old year leaves."
Bill Vaughn

"Life is too short to spend your precious time trying to convince a person who wants to live in gloom and doom otherwise. Give lifting that person your best shot, but don't hang around long enough for his or her bad attitude to pull you down. Instead, surround yourself with optimistic people."
Zig Ziglar

"There are always flowers for those who want to see them."
Henri Mattise

"Positive things happen to positive people."
Sarah Beeny

"Miracles happen every day. Not just in remote country villages or at holy sites halfway across the globe, but here, in our own lives."
Deepak Chopra

"Whatever qualities the rich may have, they can be acquired by anyone with the tenacity to become rich. The key, I think, is confidence. Confidence and an unshakable belief it can be done and that you are the one to do it."
Felix Dennis

"Leaders need to be optimists. Their vision is beyond the present."
Rudy Giuliani

"We would accomplish many more things if we did not think of them as impossible."
Vince Lombardi

"Anything's possible if you've got enough nerve."
J.K Rowling

Chapter 10

Success Quotes

"They can because they think they can."
Virgil

"Failures do what is tension relieving, while winners do what is goal achieving."
Dennis Waitley

"The talent of success is nothing more than doing what you can do, well."
Henry W. Longfellow

"The man who makes a success of an important venture never wails for the crowd. He strikes out for himself. It takes nerve, it takes a great lot of grit; but the man that succeeds has both. Anyone can fail. The public admires the man who has enough confidence in himself to take a chance. These chances are the main things after all. The man who tries to succeed must expect to be criticized. Nothing important was ever done but the greater number consulted previously doubted the possibility. Success is the accomplishment of that which most people think can't be done."
C. V. White

"I was slightly cynical of the American mentality before I came over here, but now I preach it. Here, no one's going to tear you down if you buy yourself a $300,000 car. They're likely to say: "Well, you probably worked hard for it. Good luck to you."
Simon Cowell

"Once I began following my own instincts, sales took off and I became a millionaire. And that, I think, is a key secret to every person's success, be they male or female, banker or pornographer: Trust in your gut."
Larry Flint

"Success doesn't come to you, you go to it."
Marva Collins

"Unless you're willing to have a go, fail miserably, and have another go, success won't happen."
Phillip Adams

"To laugh often and much; to win the respect of intelligent people and the affection of children...to leave the world a better place...to know even one life has breathed easier because you have lived. This is to have succeeded."
Ralph Waldo Emerson

"Striving for success without hard work is like trying to harvest where you haven't planted"
David Bly

"The first step toward success is taken when you refuse to be a captive of the environment in which you first find yourself."
Mark Caine

"A leaf that is destined to grow large is full of grooves and wrinkles at the start. Now if one has no patience and wants it smooth offhand like a willow leaf, there is trouble ahead."
Johann Wolfgang von Goethe

"For true success ask yourself these four questions: Why? Why not? Why not me? Why not now? "
James Allen

"Action is the foundational key to all success"
Pablo Picasso

"Formal education will make you a living; self-education will make you a fortune."
Jim Rohn

"I've failed over and over and over again in my life and that is why I succeed."
Michael Jordan

"Success is a lousy teacher. It seduces smart people into thinking they can't lose."
Bill Gates

Chapter 11

Time Quotes

"Men talk of killing time, while time quietly kills them."
Dion Boucicault

"Time is free, but it's priceless. You can't own it, but you can use it. You can't keep it, but you can spend it. Once you've lost it you can never get it back."
Harvey Mackay

"Yesterday is a canceled check; tomorrow is a promissory note; today is the only cash you have - so spend it wisely"
Kay Lyons

"Today is the tomorrow you worried about yesterday"
Dale Carnegie

"A man who dares to waste one hour of life has not discovered the value of life."
Charles Darwin

"Perhaps the very best question that you can memorize and repeat, over and over, is, "what is the most valuable use of my time right now?"
Brian Tracy

"Defer no time, delays have dangerous ends."
William Shakespeare

"Time is the coin of your life. It is the only coin you have, and only you can determine how it will be spent. Be careful lest you let other people spend it for you."
Carl Sandburg

"You may delay, but time will not."
Benjamin Franklin

"Time is an equal opportunity employer. Each human being has exactly the same number of hours and minutes every day. Rich people can't buy more hours. Scientists can't invent new minutes. And you can't save time to spend it on another day. Even so, time is amazingly fair and forgiving. No matter how much time you've wasted in the past, you still have an entire tomorrow."
Denis Waitely

"Time is a great teacher, but unfortunately it kills all its pupils."
Louis Hector Berlioz

"Time heals what reason cannot"
Seneca

"Much may be done in those little shreds and patches of time which every day produces, and which most men throw away."
Charles Caleb Colton

"Waste your money and you're only out of money, but waste your time and you've lost a part of your life."
Michael LeBoeuf

"You can do so much in 10 minutes' time .Ten minutes, once gone, are gone for good. Divide your life into 10-minute units and sacrifice as few of them as possible in meaningless activity."
Ingvar Kamprad

"Time = life; therefore, waste your time and waste of your life, or master your time and master your life."
Alan Lakein

"Don't be fooled by the calendar. There are only as many days in the year as you make use of. One man gets only a week's value out of a year while another man gets a full year's value out of a week."
Charles Richards

"The time for action is now. It's never too late to do something."
Carl Sandburg